Carlos Gimeno

Public Speaking

A Very Practical Introduction

Public Speaking: A Very Practical Introduction

Carlos Gimeno

Written and Published by Carlos Gimeno

Printed by Ingram Spark

Edited by Alison Macfarlane

Text and Cover Design by Sancho Dean

ISBN-13: 978-1-5272-5879-2

Table of Contents

Table of Contents

The Bonus Material

Why Does This Book Exist?

The British say "Thank you" a lot. Although I am not British by birth or by passport, I have lived on British soil long enough to make this custom my own. Thank you for investing two of your most valuable commodities – your money and time – in this book. I am confident that you won't regret either.

This book is a practical reference for anyone interested in self-improvement, of which public speaking represents a significant contribution. Public speaking is often, mistakenly, thought of as just the grand speeches of politicians and famous artists. But there are many other examples of public speaking, including presentations, meetings, conversations, your family breakfast talk and the small chat of a dinner party. And that is why I have decided to share my experiences with you in a concise and practical way: so that you can gradually and easily improve the way you interact verbally with other human beings.

Most books published on public speaking have a focus on business or on TED Talks-style speeches (https://www.ted.com/talks). This book is for people like you and I, and it takes a very practical approach. Its details can be applied to everyday–life situations.

The benefit for you is in learning ten basic principles that will assist in polishing the structure and the style of your verbal communication. I use Public Speaking in the title and throughout the book as a synonym for verbal communication, since all communication interactions you have outside a one-to-one conversation can and should be classified as Public Speaking.

The text is based on dozens of interactions I have had with other individuals, groups and audiences in the UK, Europe, the United States, Africa, Asia and Latin America. And it is also based on dozens of mistakes I have made in the process – mistakes you can avoid by reading this book. It is written as an introduction for those starting out on a journey of self-awareness and self-improvement, as well as a useful reminder for those who have already mastered some of the basic skills.

Thank you and enjoy the read!

A Note About Carlos

I am an optimist and a liberal. I am a dreamer and a history-lover. I am not a politician. I am not an evangelist. And I don't know everything. I am a journalist by training and a salesman by trade and I enjoy public speaking more than almost everything else in life, hence the book. I am an average bloke speaking, writing and sharing from personal experience so that others can benefit, avoid the mistakes I have made and progress faster in life.

I have had the pleasure and the privilege to enjoy 14 years of my life in the quintessential English city of Oxford, where I am still based. My public speaking journey began 16 years ago while presenting an English language learning course to a group of Spanish primary school teachers. The excitement, the fun, the need and desire to improve and advance my personal and professional achievement have never stopped since.

2010 was a turning point in my public speaking adventure, as I discovered and joined the Oxford

Speakers Club (OSC). A great proportion of my improvement, passion and the experiences shared in this book are a consequence of my OSC life and I am extremely grateful to them for the doors of knowledge and discovery they have opened for me.

The Oxford Speakers Club

The Oxford Speakers Club belongs to Toastmasters International (www.toastmasters.org), a charitable organisation that has been helping people like you and me improve their communication skills for more than 90 years.

The Fabulous Team Behind This Gem

Acknowledgements in books are an annoyance in all of them – except for those individuals whose names are listed in them! So, if you are certain that you haven't contributed to this book in any way, I won't be offended if you jump to the start of the book and begin learning. For those of you who have made a contribution, keep on reading for your dose of free printed gratitude and recognition.

The first "Thank you" goes to the three gorgeous, talented and generous individuals who appear with me in the photo here: Alison, Sancho and Laura. They have transformed a piece of meat into a delicious and digestible meal. Thank you!

Secondly, I must mention my friends, the friends who, without promise of any financial reward, accepted my requests for input, feedback and advice. Especially Julia Harris and Adele Parker. I am grateful to you both for being you, for being there and for being helpful.

Finally, I want to thank the many inspirational people I have met over the years, both in my publishing career and in my Toastmasters life. You all have been a source of improvement and education, and directly or indirectly, your advice and insights have become a part of this book's DNA. Thank you all!

Sancho – Designer

I'm a inquisitive introvert from South London, with a great love for Graphics and spicy food. Hoping to trade Carlos creative ideas on his projects, (including this book, which I have helped format and cover) for tips on public speaking (not that I get out from behind my computer screen much). I've spent the last five years developing fast fashion prints for global retailers, which has helped fund my passion for exploring countries with better weather and cheaper alcohol. Although considered precocious by the lady I am blessed to call mother, most would probably describe me as a pessimistically humorous individual. I'm a younger brother to two amazing sisters who thrive being on stage, which has lead me to often question my laid back and slightly shy personality.

Laura – Illustrator

I was born in 1987 in Provence, in the south of France, where I've spent most of my life. I went on to study English literature and civilisation in Aix-en-Provence, but always had a growing passion for art, which I worked on as a hobby. After travelling for a year in Australia, I moved to Oxford, where I met Carlos through work. I created a painting for him, which led to our collaboration on this book. I'm now living a peaceful life in north Cornwall, working as an Ayurvedic massage therapist at a local spa, and still doing a few bits of art on the side.

Alison – Editor

I'm passionate about words and how you can use them to draw an amazing and vivid picture. I love reading fiction, as at its best it not only tells a fantastic story but also showcases language as a work of art. So when Carlos asked me to cast my editorial eye over his book on public speaking – itself a celebration of the power of words – I jumped at the chance. With my nose in a book ever since I could read, I went on to study English and American literature at university before becoming a bookseller in Oxford. I then pursued a career in publishing in Oxford and London. Raising two boys into young men whilst working at home, I've recently taken on a new position as a production editor in academic publishing.

'The team on a day out in Bath, from left to right: Sancho, Laura, Alison and Carlos'

Photographer - Guy Traynor
www.guytraynorphoto.com

Part 1: The Basics

Chapter 1

The 1. 2. 3 Rule

Whatever message, story, idea, concept or feeling you are trying to convey, the simplest method is to split it into three blocks or chunks of text: Introduction, Body and Conclusion. This applies when you are communicating both verbally or in writing, whether at a wedding, a corporate meeting or a job interview.

Life is complicated enough. When it comes to communicating, clarity, brevity, conciseness and what I call brutal simplicity of thought are essential. The human brain operates in complex and mysterious ways, and we often make the mistake of letting it loose. The inevitable consequence is a breathless, tired and confused audience who, unable to follow your thoughts, switch off. Having witnessed this phenomenon countless times, I propose the 1.2.3 Rule as an easy, safe and efficient solution.

1. Introduction

More often than I would have liked I have seen even relatively experienced speakers and presenters making the mistake of throwing themselves into the core of their subject. They don't even explain what the topic is, why it is relevant to the speaker **and the audience (!)** or what the proposed initiative, outcome or solution is.

Let me break this down in more detail. Generally, audiences are varied, preoccupied, multi-cultural and multi-lingual, and aren't necessarily familiar with you or the subject you are speaking about. You can't make any assumptions and you mustn't take anything for granted. You must try and use what I call "baby language". The best introductions I have heard in public speeches tend to be made of short sentences with powerful language and at least one pause of two to three seconds.

By the way, your introduction shouldn't be longer than one paragraph, or six sentences. It needs to be confident and strong. In the first two or three sentences, you should state who you are, and if time allows it, add a few words about yourself and your background. You should then say what the subject of your speech is. The last two or three sentences should contain the reason behind your presence and your speech.

> *"Why am I here? Why is what I am about to tell you relevant, interesting and important? And, above all, why should you listen to me?!"*

There are several ways of doing this.

- You can describe a problem or a challenge and how it is affecting people's lives.

- You can also quote statistics or figures to illustrate your point, but don't quote too many as numbers are difficult to remember and can put listeners off.

- You can tell a brief story about someone you know, someone close to you, or even about yourself!

- Rhetorical questions or direct questions to the audience are also a powerful way to get you started.

The pace in these initial words is ideally slower than your usual speaking pace and should be crowned by a strong, powerful, confident pause. I will talk about pauses and silence in speeches in more detail in Chapter 7 but I will say now that the power of meaningful and purposeful pauses cannot be emphasised enough. This first pause at the end of your speech introduction will give your audience a clear and strong signal about your confidence and the importance of what you are about to say. It's a bit like saying, "Fasten your seat belts, we are about to go on an exciting ride!" It will also give them time to process and digest what you have just said and make any necessary physical and mental adjustments as you begin with the body of your speech.

2. The Body

One of the biggest challenges for any speaker is to be able to maintain the audience's attention during the core of the speech. This is true whether it's a five-minute speech or a half an hour speech. Although, obviously and inevitably, the longer the speech, the more challenging keeping listeners' interest becomes. Introductions and conclusions tend to be shorter and easier to remember and therefore easier to deliver. They also take place when the audience's attention is at its highest. This is certainly true of the introduction. It may not be so true of the conclusion, but in a well-structured and well-delivered speech, the audience will feel that the end is approaching and so their minds and bodies will prepare themselves for that climax. The central part of any speech is certainly harder to sustain and therefore requires more preparatory work and attention. My key recommendation is to apply the **1. 2. 3 Rule** you are using for the whole of the speech to the middle part of the speech itself. Whatever the subject, it can be and should be broken down into no more than three key elements (stories) to help you illustrate and explain your point. The speaker needs to make this division clear to the audience. You can signal the transition from one point to the next either by numbering them, or by making it clear with your language variety and use of connector words. As well as personal experiences (more on this in the next chapter), it is also advisable to make use of questions and vocal variety to keep your audience awake.

At this point in the book I must reiterate my obsession with the use of pauses and silence in public speaking. They are an extremely important piece of the jigsaw when it comes to the body of the speech, and I will offer some key tips and cover them with more passion in Chapter 7.

3. Conclusion

A good speech cannot be such without a good, succinct, powerful and thought-provoking finale. The two go hand in hand, just like marrying a fine wine with a meal, matching the perfect suit with a tie and a pair of shoes, the icing on the cake and the biscuit with your mid-afternoon cup of tea. Ironically though, a good conclusion starts in the introduction. What I mean by this is that for you to naturally finish off your speech you need to make sure that you have built enough expectation, interest, curiosity and anticipation in both the introduction and the body. How efficiently and clearly you can do this depends to some extent on the subject matter and the flow of the speech. Storytelling facilitates such progression more easily and more naturally than, say, a technical or commercial speech that is dominated by facts and figures.

There are a number of things you can do to build in that climactic sensation and make sure that the last few sentences of your speech are just a welcome, natural and effortless final step.

- Announcing or hinting during the body of the speech that the end is near is one possible way of doing so.

- Referring to a secret ingredient, reason or solution that will be revealed and shared at the end is another option.

- Accelerating your pace and volume as you approach the end works quite well to achieve this effect, too.

Looking at the conclusion itself, it shouldn't be longer than the introduction. In fact, if possible, it should be shorter. It must be signalled at the start of it either by a pause or by language – or both. Like the introduction, it benefits from having a strong, confident, thought-provoking and please-give-me more tone and feel to it.

So, keep it simple, and split whatever you are saying into three parts. Make the end punchy and try and close with a quote or a memorable sentence.

Thinking About Thanking

There are different opinions about whether a speech should end with a "Thank you" to the audience. There are those purists who say that it shouldn't. They argue that the audience is there because they want to be and it is they who should be thanking the speaker! Others believe that a "Thank you" at the end of your speech is not only a polite and clear way to bring your show to an end. It also allows the speaker to culminate his or her performance and make that clear to the audience too. My view is that it depends on the circumstances, the type of speech, the context and how successful the speaker feels the speech has been. My preference is to avoid it where possible. But I recognise that it can work well in more formal scenarios, such as corporate presentations and political rallies.

'The golden rule of 3'

Chapter 2

The Less is More Rule

Most people faced with the challenge of writing and delivering a speech will be asking themselves how much writing they will need to do to fill the speaking time they have been given. And most of the time, they will feel the urge to write a lot – having lots of content provides the speaker with a sense of comfort and confidence. This is an illusion. The more content you have, the more difficult it is to keep a clear structure and the faster you will need to speak. The faster you speak, the less authority you retain, and your audience will be lost and confused.

> *"I have heard and delivered enough speeches to know that when it comes to public speaking less is more."*

In fact, the shorter the written version of your speech is, the clearer it will be. Its brief physical nature will allow you to keep control of all the other elements we will cover in this book. My experience tells me that you only need an A4 sheet (or one page) to cover five minutes of your spoken speech.

Assuming a fairly regular spoken rhythm, a 1.2.3 structure (remember the previous chapter?), a few pauses and a relative simplicity of thought, this can be compounded as follows:

10 minutes = two pages

15 minutes = three pages

20 minutes = four pages

And so on and so forth.

A note of caution though, any speech longer than 30 minutes should be approached with a slightly different writing technique. Your capacity to speak at the same speed for that length of time, and the audience's ability to follow you, are limited. So perhaps you should reduce the writing/speaking ratio to one and a half pages for every 10 minutes and support your delivery with visual aids and longer, more purposeful silences (as I've already mentioned, more on silences and the effective use of pauses in Chapter 7).

One page of written material should be enough to convey your message clearly and concisely in five minutes. It also gives you and the audience time for questions and for clarifying any points that require expanding. A further benefit of this approach, and crucial from a delivery point of view, is the fact that having your five-minute speech on one page allows you to take a mental picture of it. You can prepare for its verbal delivery, remembering key pointers and sentences that will then keep you on track, to give the speech a natural and easy-to-follow flow.

The Less is More Rule is especially useful, and necessary, in the case of highly emotionally charged speeches, like those for weddings and other family reunions. And also in highly complex and technical presentations where brevity and clarity will keep the audience listening. Speeches where a faster rhythm may be a good thing, such as story speeches and professional and commercial talks, may require longer texts.

The success in implementing The Less is More Rule depends on how fast you speak, so give it a go to see how you do. Write one page of content on something you are interested in and practice delivering it within a five-minute slot. If you finish your spoken delivery in under four minutes you are speaking too fast. If you go over five minutes and 30 seconds, you are speaking too slowly and need to try again! (More on pace and its consequences in Chapter 4.)

***

So you now have one page of written material for every five minutes you need to speak for and you have the whole speech, irrespective of its length, split into three parts. It's now time to build your story.

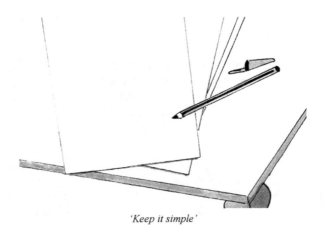

'Keep it simple'

Chapter 3

Storyology

Once you have identified the physical length of your speech and its structure it is time to think about the tone and the nature of your words. Even in technical and commercial presentations, the golden rule for grabbing your audience's attention and keeping it through the speech is to tell a story. And if it is a personal one, that is even better.

The things that bind us together and cross barriers of class, wealth, status, nationality and religion (or the lack of it) are experiences and feelings. It doesn't matter how rich or poor or religious we are, we are all exposed at some point in our lives to similar experiences and to the same feelings (such as happiness, anger, sadness, thirst, hunger, etc.).

So drawing from your own experiences and feelings to carry your speech is a very effective way to connect with your audience. It allows them to empathise with you and, more importantly, to listen to you and remember what you say. And the best way to do this is to frame those experiences and feelings into a story. Handily, a story tends to support the structure described in the first chapter and will in fact help you to create it. Needless to say, the story must be true.

You could make up a fantastically powerful and emotional story to convey your message but, unless you are a professional actor, the likelihood is that the audience will realise early in the speech that it is not your story. This would have devastating consequences for your credibility both at the moment of delivery and in the future, as well as for your speech's success.

In addition to strengthening your message, the story-telling style will help you remember your own words. It gives you more time, and allows you to focus on the delivery elements of your performance that will contribute to an overall more polished product. These elements include vocal variety and body language, both of which I'll tell you more about later in the book.

If you don't have any relevant stories of your own, it is acceptable to tell stories that have been lived and experienced by those close to you, such as friends, relatives and even work colleagues. Or the story of someone you don't know but which has made a big impact on you and that you consider relevant and supportive of your message. When doing so, however, you may need to dedicate a few more words in your introduction to the background to the story and why you have chosen it. When telling other people's stories, I would, as a courtesy, ask for the protagonist's permission to share it, particularly if your speech is being filmed.

Telling a story will guarantee a slicker performance. It will make you more credible, more likeable, more fun to watch and listen to and easier to remember. Practice it in some other of your life's everyday situations, such as meals with the family, work meetings and friends' reunions, and you will discover its power.

In addition to powerful introductions and endings, two of the key components of stories are characters and dialogue. As you write and prepare your speech, spend time and words on describing the key characters in your story (there shouldn't be more than three or four). Describe their personalities and context and then bring them alive to the audience by paraphrasing or reproducing their dialogues. Both the characters' descriptions and the dialogues should be included in the first part of the body of the speech.

***

One final recommendation on telling stories. The best stories are those that combine happy and sad moments. The twists and turns in your story will contribute to building a sense of suspense. They will keep your audience wanting more (see the last chapter to learn more on "feeding your audience") and will give the speech a natural and real flow. If you make your audience laugh and cry within the same speech, you literally have them in your hands.

'Stories help us remember'

Brutally Concise Summary of Part 1

Congratulations! You have reached the end of Part 1 of the most important book you will ever read. Because the human memory is selective (not limited!); because you have a million other things in your brain that keep you happy and alive more efficiently than this book; and because a part of learning happens through repetition and simplification, here is a delightfully (and brutally) brief summary of what you have read and learnt so far:

*   Keep your message simple and **ALWAYS** divide your speech into **THREE PARTS**: Introduction, Body and Conclusion.

*   Keep your message short: you need just **ONE A4** page to speak for **FIVE MINUTES**. If you have more to say, keep it for a future speech.

*   Keep it personal and **TELL A STORY**: the closer to reality and to yourself the better. **CHARACTERS** and **DIALOGUE** will enhance the story's engagement and credibility. Introduce them in the first part of the body of the speech.

Part 2: The Complements

Chapter 4

Mind Your Speed

So now you are in the thick of it. You have the A4 sheets of your speech in your head, you have divided it into three easy-to-remember parts and you have given it a personal story that will keep your audience hooked. Excellent. Next, you need to mind your speed.

In my first ever speech at the Oxford Speakers Club (known in Toastmasters terminology as the Ice-Breaker) I was given very useful feedback by the club members. Feedback and evaluations are central to the Toastmasters culture as well as an integral part of anyone's public speaking journey. Amongst their comments, one stayed in my head and I have applied it to my speeches ever since. The faster you speak, the more difficult it is for your audience to follow you, and the more rushed and out-of-control your speech comes across.

There are a few exceptions to this, which I will cover in Chapter 6. Conversely, the slower you speak (within limits!) the more in control you appear to be. You gain more authority as someone who knows the subject and can communicate it in a controlled, well-paced, calm manner. Nervousness and excitement can become your enemies as you try to achieve this composed image, and the body's tendency is to accelerate itself as the speech progresses. At this point I need to refer to the importance of pauses again (see more in Chapter 7). Well-timed, long enough pauses will help you achieve the desired pace and reinforce that sense of control and gravitas. This in turn will make your audience feel relaxed and comfortable about both your experience and theirs.

As with most things in life, taking this to the extreme could cause the opposite effect. If you end up speaking too slowly and your natural pitch happens to be low and difficult to hear you will lose the audience's attention. Your speech will lack the energy and enthusiasm required to keep it engaging. We all speak at different speeds and what may sound fast to some could seem incredibly slow to others. You just need to find a pace that you feel comfortable with and that allows you to deliver your speech within the allocated time.

Another effective way to find your pace is to ask for feedback from audience members.

"Ask for feedback every time you give a speech or whenever you conduct a meeting or do a job interview."

Remember, as I said in the introduction, public speaking doesn't only happen at political rallies or at the United Nations or at a conference. It happens in most daily activities – whether we notice it or not. So the opportunity to ask for feedback, input, advice and comments from your interlocutors is always available. Everyday. Everywhere.

If in doubt about the speed of your speech, opt for a slower delivery. It will help you keep calm, and your audience (and their brains and ears) will thank you for it. The exceptions are inspirational and persuasive speeches, which require a faster pace, or at least a combination of fast and slow.

***

It is also worth noting as a final reminder in this chapter that the speed of your speech is directly related to its physical length (remember the The Less is More Rule in Chapter 2?). And to how much and how well you have rehearsed it, which I will expand upon in Chapter 8. This becomes more and more important and relevant as you improve and make progress in your public speaking journey. Synchronising all these elements as you become more confident is essential for a successful final product.

'The slower the better'

Chapter 5

Speak With Your Body

I am not going to bore you with scientific or academic quotes, which you are likely to forget by the time you have finished reading this chapter. Instead, I will start this part of the book by sharing something I heard, as it happens, in a speech. It was about the balance between what we say (the words we speak) and how we say them (their actual delivery). And the impact seeing and listening to those words has on the audience. The speaker I am referring to said that the vast majority of the impact of your speech depends on its delivery.

Only a tiny proportion of what the audience remembers is a direct consequence of the actual words. The key component of any performance is your body: its presence, its look and how you use it – hopefully, to your advantage.

Body language, as it is commonly referred to, is crucial in your success as a speaker. You must become comfortable with playing and experimenting with your body language and using your body to speak, too. Whether we like it or not, we make more decisions than we think based on the information we receive from our brain and through our eyes. Consequently, an audience makes an initial judgment on the speaker as soon as she or he goes up on the stage, purely based on what they look like. I know this is unfair and irrational, but it is true. And the analysis will constantly continue, sometimes unconsciously, as you move your body to reinforce your message. Unless you work as a performer, only your upper body will be visible to your audience in most public speaking experiences in your life. So I am going to focus in this chapter on the eyes and the hands.

The Two Most Sophisticated Communication Tools on Earth

Our vision is one of our key senses and our eyes are one of the main receptors of information from the outside world. They also allow us to connect with other fellow human beings, express feelings and show and reinforce intentions. They therefore become a priceless tool to use when trying to engage successfully with your audience. It doesn't matter whether your eyes are blue, green or orange, big or small, round or flat. The first thing they will help you do, irrespective of their shape or colour, is to make and maintain eye contact with your audience. Many speakers of all levels make the mistake of fixing their eyes, and therefore their attention, on just a small area of a room or something in it, or only a small segment of the audience, maybe even just one person. The consequence of this is that you are immediately losing the rest of the audience as well as your own awareness of what is happening elsewhere in the room.

I understand and know from first-hand experience how difficult it is to keep good eye contact with everyone in the audience (or all segments of it if you have a large one) while trying to remember your words, maintain a relatively low and authoritative pace and keep within the time limits. But it is important to work on it and make it a habit. The more eye contact you make with your audience the more connected you are with them. The greater the weight and the impact of your words the stronger the emotional commitment will be. Maintaining eye contact is fun to practice when you are in a meeting at work or talking with a group of friends.

As with all the other ideas I am sharing in this book,

success comes with practice. But it is worth knowing that half of that major delivery impact I quoted earlier depends on how well you use your eyes. The other half comes from your hands.

The Two Most Powerful Communication Tools on Earth

We mostly think of our hands as extensions of our arms. Tools to grab, handle and hold objects, instruments, vehicles. Not many of us think of them, at least not consciously, as communication tools. Well, they happen to be a pair of very efficient ones. The way you decide to use or not to use your hands during any act of communication becomes an important way to convey your message successfully. Hand movements in public speaking can be used to emphasise, dramatise or illustrate. If your hand movements aren't supporting any of these primary objectives, don't use them. My advice would be to keep them by your sides or gracefully and discreetly in front of you, either clasping them or in a triangle shape.

Using hands for emphasis is characteristically easy to observe in politicians, particularly politicians with big hands, such as Bill Clinton. As well as highlighting a point or a policy statement, using your hands adds a sense of confidence and control that reinforces such emphasis. I would recommend using them regularly in your speeches, during the central part of your speech as you outline the two or three key elements of your story. When it comes to dramatising, or illustrating a point, using your hands to support your words is particularly useful. It allows your audience to see as well as hear your words. It also makes your delivery look more natural and smooth, as well as making it easier for your audience to follow.

Whether it is counting numbers, demonstrating an action or performing a move or an exercise, using your hands makes a greater impact than words by themselves. It also gives you a break from the rigidity that doing nothing with your hands can give your look and delivery. The use of the index finger to address a crowd or point to something or someone and the use of fist gestures can both be particularly powerful and supportive of your message.

Hand movements, and body language in general, must be purposeful (including walking onto and away from the stage). The sacred rule is that if your body language is not supporting or adding value to your words in any way you shouldn't try to speak with your body! Regular and strategically planned body language is a key component of any polished performance. Purposeless, irregular (erratic) and unplanned body language will damage the smoothness of your delivery, your credibility and your confidence as well as the audience's ability to follow you and listen to and remember your words. As we will see in Chapter 8, achieving this depends greatly on practice and preparation.

***

My final note on this subject and chapter is related to the points made in the previous chapter about speed. Some of your movements will need to be faster than others, especially when you are using them to add emphasis or drama. But the safest rule when it comes to how quickly to move is to make controlled, relatively slow and smooth movements. This gives those listening (and watching) time to connect your movements with the very words they are supporting or complementing and to digest and take in the fullness of your message or point.

Nixon vs. Kennedy Presidential Debate

A fantastic example of the importance of body language in public speaking is the Nixon vs. Kennedy presidential debate in 1960, which I encourage you to watch. An interesting analysis of the different perceptions about who had won the debate amongst those who watched the televised edition and those who listened to it on the radio is both fascinating and revealing of the importance of the relationship between words and actions.

'Your two most powerful communication tools'

Chapter 6

Let Them Hear You

We speak to be heard. We speak to be listened to. We speak to communicate. We speak to express, share, warn, inform, inspire, persuade, entertain and even sometimes, unfortunately, to threaten and scare. None of these actions can be successfully executed unless you are physically heard. And so, your voice and how you use it is one of the most vital parts of any verbal public appearance. The strength with which you project your voice, its variety of tone and pitch and its volume, rhythm and pace are all key. Getting your voice's volume right, in particular, is very important. Shout and you will alienate, whisper and you will be ignored.

There are two factors that determine which way (high or low) you should go with your voice.

The first one is the venue. The bigger the room you are in, the louder your volume should be. It is also important to consider your distance from the audience. If in addition to being in a large location there are several metres between you and your audience, you will need to turn up your volume. The closer you are to your audience, the easier it is for them to hear you and so you can adopt a lower voice. Both situations will also be influenced by technical circumstances, such as whether you are provided with a microphone. If you are using a microphone, it is advisable to perform a volume test before your audience arrives.

The second element to consider as you try to decide how loud or quiet your voice should be is the size of the audience. In principle, the bigger the group, the more effort your voice needs to make to reach all the people.

As with many other aspects of public speaking, getting your voice right becomes easier with practice. And like with many other things in life, you are bound to make a few mistakes along the way. Unlike the speed of your speech, with the volume of your voice it is better to be too loud than too quiet. If you are too loud, at least your audience will get to hear what you have to say, even if their ears hurt a little by the end! Irrespective of venue and audience size, it is also a good idea to play with different voices throughout your speech. You can adjust your volume as you go along if the audience's body language tells you are speaking either too loudly or too quietly.

***

Finally, and this is incredibly useful when used in conjunction with purposeful and planned body language, combine high and low pitches to keep your audience engaged, interested and awake! Pitch variation is very useful as an impact and surprise resource: go low to add intimacy, privacy or sadness and go high to try and increase drama, reinforce violence and strength or just to enact a loud scene as part of your story. This vocal variety will not only contribute to the naturalness of your delivery, but will also increase engagement and impact. The bottom line is that you are speaking in public to be heard, so let them hear you!!

'Turn the volume up'

Chapter 7

Enjoy The Silence

This is highly likely to be the most important chapter of this book, and it is, ironically, a chapter on silence! It is at this point that I would like you to stop reading for a few seconds and hear the silence around you.

Nice, isn't it? Hearing and enjoying the silence is extremely important because there isn't much of it in the world or in our lives. As with so many other elements that aren't available in abundance, it becomes valuable, rare, welcome, comforting, unique, desired, stylish, distinguished, elegant and, yes, enjoyable. This lack-based value applies to speech-craft with very powerful consequences when it is used skilfully and purposefully, and with devastating consequences when not used at all.

In some parts of this chapter I am going to use silence and pauses as synonyms, even though silence in a speech is simply the consequence of a pause. So I will continue to write as though they are the same thing. I will also take a pause in a speech to mean a deliberate interruption that is longer than one second.

Pauses are not just important but essential in any speech because:

1. They provide your delivery with an aura of gravitas, control, eloquence, intrigue, sophistication and a "give me more, please" reaction in the audience that sets your speech apart.

2. They give you, the speaker, time to breathe, rest, think, assess and connect more deeply with your audience.

3. They give the audience time to breathe, rest, digest everything you've said so far, get ready for what you are about to say next and connect more deeply with you.

4. They balance the speed of your speech.

5. They facilitate vocal variety.

6. They facilitate transitions between ideas and parts of your speech and story.

7. They fill the room.

8. They allow you to address anything that might be going wrong. You may need a sip of water, to adjust a piece of clothing that is distracting you and the audience, to reorganise your notes (if you are using them), to check (very discreetly, almost invisibly) the time you have left or myriad other issues.

9. Particularly in story-telling and personal speeches, they build intensity, drama, emotion and anticipation.

10. They feel, look and sound good.

As with all elements of public speaking, mastering silences and their use in a speech comes with practice – and lots of it. I recommend starting with one or two silences and adding more as your speeches become longer and more complex. The number of pauses is directly proportional to the length of the speech. But I wouldn't recommend having more than three or four long ones (around three to five seconds) in a speech of up to 15 minutes.

> *"You can of course play with the number of pauses you have and how long they are. You could, for example, have two short ones (around two to three seconds) and two long ones or three short ones and a (very) long one (over six seconds) within the same speech."*

All this depends on what you are using pauses for and when. And this takes me to my next point, which is what I call the silence's purposefulness. To understand this concept, and the use and need of pauses in speeches in general, I encourage you to witness the longest and most powerful silence I have seen or heard in a public speech, ever! It happened during a United Nations address by Israeli Prime Minister Benjamin Netanyahu in 2016 – type "Netanyahu long silence at United Nations" in Google to see the video.

Make sure you don't use pauses just for the sake of it. They ought to have a purpose, as outlined in my list of benefits, above. If they don't have a purpose, they may come across as artificial and unnecessary stops that break the flow of the speech. So, yes, pauses are important, but you need to give some thought as to why and where in the speech you are using them.

As you make your first steps in public speaking, an easy way to develop a habit of including pauses in your speeches is to mark them up as you write your words down, whether you intend to use notes during your delivery or not. If you are using notes in your delivery writing the pauses in will help you remember them. If you aren't going to use notes during the actual delivery, it will still help you to practice your pauses and give them a spontaneity and naturalness when you rehearse your speech (more on this on the next chapter). You can make these marks in any shape or form or colour that helps you remember them. I have always favoured big red dots.

***

One of the best ways to understand the need for pauses and the consequences of not using them is to witness a speech without them. As we close this very important chapter, and so you can digest its enormity, take a moment to stop reading and ENJOY the silence... :)

'Powerful, priceless silence'

Brutally Concise Summary of Part 2

You now have seven of the most precious pieces of advice in public speaking history. And you are about to have exclusive access to three more. Before you do so, I don't want you to forget what you have learnt so far, so here is the second of my brutally concise summaries:

- Keep an eye on your speed: the **SLOWER** you speak (within limits!) the more **GRAVITAS** and **AUTHORITY** you and your speech will gain.

- Keep using your **EYES** and **HANDS** purposefully in speeches to support your words. If gestures don't support what you're saying, well, stop them!

- Keep a **VARIED TONE AND VOLUME** of voice: play with highs and lows depending on the emotions you are communicating. Be aware of venue and audience size when doing so.

- Keep in mind that **PAUSES ARE ABSOLUTELY ESSENTIAL** to your speaking success: play with them and include them in all speeches. See my list as a reminder of all the benefits.

Part 3: The Final Touches

Chapter 8

The PPP Rule

Whether we call it the "Practice, Practice, Practice" rule or the "Preparation, Preparation, Preparation" rule or the "Perseverance, Perseverance, Perseverance" rule – you get the point! I would say that around three quarters of your success when delivering a speech depends on the amount of time spent on rehearsing your delivery – assuming you have mastered all the other elements covered so far in this book.

To feel confident when the time comes to stand up and speak and to have the mental capacity to coordinate all the points addressed so far and react to any changes, crises or unforeseen circumstances, you need to be ready to deliver. The only way to gain this confidence is to practice, practice, practice.

It is not a good idea to memorise the whole speech, as if you do rely entirely on memory, forgetting a single word could be catastrophic. My advice when practising your speech is simply to go through it several times as close to the actual delivery as possible. You should do this at least five times for a five-minute speech but there is no limit – the more times the better!

Practising your speech will help you to reduce nerves. I am deliberately using the word "reduce" because nerves will never disappear completely and nor should they anyway. Practice key pauses and hand gestures and make amendments and improvements as you hear the actual words you have written and can see and hear your speech all as one piece. Certain sentences, words and even some pauses can look and sound great in isolation, as you write your speech sentence-by-sentence and paragraph-by-paragraph. But they may not sound good at all as they blend with the rest of the speech.

Another massive benefit of this pre-delivery exercise is that it will tell you exactly how accurate your timing is. It is one thing to read a speech from a piece of paper at home and a very different thing to actually say the words in front of an audience. Unless you are a very experienced or cold-blooded speaker, your pace is bound to be faster and, as a consequence, your overall timing shorter, than when you read it and practice alone. So when you practice in the comfort of your living-room, bathroom, garden or wherever you are, you will not only need to make any necessary adjustments to the structure of the speech, but also to the length of some sentences and paragraphs and the use and location of pauses to anticipate your speedier "live" delivery.

The more you have practiced **and** the more you have rehearsed **and** prepared **and** persevered **and** the more comfortable and familiar you are with the transitions between the paragraphs and the words you are saying, the more confident and relaxed you will appear. And the more you and the audience will enjoy the experience. It will also give you the confidence to be spontaneous. You may want to add things that weren't in the final written version but that feel right to be added when delivering it in front of an audience, whether it is a word or phrase or a gesture or pause.

It is never a good idea to assume that both the environment and the audience will be under control while you speak. Unexpected crises do happen, so the more prepared you are, the better and the more quickly you will react when faced with difficult situations. The longer or more high-profile the speech and the bigger the audience, the more you need to prepare.

The PPP Rule

***

You can never prepare too much, but I understand that there is never enough time to practice as much as you would like either. As you become more fluent in your speech writing and delivery you will also become more efficient with your preparation time. But it doesn't matter how advanced you are, your route to success still hangs on that life-saving thread of Preparation, Preparation, Preparation.

'Practice, practice, practice'

Chapter 9

Dress For Success

The key points I need to make about this are:

- This is not a public speaking (only) rule but a rule for life.

- Dressing for success doesn't mean wearing high-heels and a skirt or a suit and a tie.

Dressing for success means wearing something you are comfortable with, feel good in and about and that enhances your natural beauty. But that is also appropriate and relevant for the context and occasion in which your speech takes place.

There is a dramatic and painful inevitability about your presence/look/image: people can see you!! And because they can see you, within the first few seconds of your appearance on stage they are going to form, consciously and unconsciously, an opinion of you based entirely on your image. And in today's world, our image is defined primarily by what we wear, including our shoes and hairstyle.

I am not saying you need to be immaculate to be eloquent, spotless to be credible, slick to be interesting, posh to be listened to and remembered. All I am saying is that dressing for success means crafting (yes, the use of the term crafting is deliberate) an image. That image has to be in harmony with who you are and what you are comfortable with, your audience's profile and values and the location and its environment. A good example of dressing for success is wearing a pair of shorts, a t-shirt and flip-flops to address the audience of a surfing competition on a beach in Australia. The same example can also be used to illustrate what dressing for failure would be. If the speaker were to wear the same outfit when delivering the keynote address at a banking conference in London, it would be a disaster. If you get the dress-success code right and have taken the PPP rule to the extremes of human capabilities, there is very little else you have to do to make your speech a real success.

***

So, pay attention to what you wear and what you look like when you put yourself in front an audience, whether at a conference, a job interview, work or the gym. Remember, you are visible wherever you are!

'Elegance is subjective'

Chapter 10

Plant a Seed

The number of similarities between public speaking and other areas of life is endless. This is certainly true with the conclusion of your speech, what taste you leave in the audience's mouth, what sensations they have and, most importantly, what actions they are compelled to take the second you pronounce your last word. The conclusion's importance and effect can be likened to the chocolate mousse at the end of a deliciously satisfying meal, the result of an exam, the climax of an orgasm, the laughter provoked by a joke.

To invoke the feeling that, with the end of your speech, something bigger and better and more special than the speech itself begins is the ultimate objective of any speaker. Whether it is inspiration, motivation, persuasion, compassion, support, understanding, humour, drama or emotions that you are trying to communicate, your speech will have an impact on those listening to it. And the final few seconds of any speech will determine the lasting impact of your performance on stage, assuming everything prior has been smooth and articulate. It is, therefore, important to spend time thinking about how you are going to conclude your speech, which words you are going to use and what the final message or call to action is going to be.

There are three key boxes to tick in any speech finale:

1. Summarise the key points of your speech

We remember faster and better by repetition. You don't want to, and quite simply can't, in the last few sentences, go again through everything you have said in a 25-minute, or even a five-minute, speech. But you must recap on the core two or three messages you have addressed. If you don't, it doesn't matter how well you have delivered them, they may well be forgotten.

2. Finish with a call to action/final statement

Because of the way our brains and memory work, your audience is going to forget a lot of the actual content of your speech. You want them to, at least, remember the central message you are sharing with them. Not only do you want them to remember it, but also to take it away with them and, ideally, to share it with others, too. To achieve this you need to come up with a memorable quote that helps you do precisely that, to plant a seed in their minds that grows over time. This can be something you've written yourself, or it can be borrowed from someone else.

3. Leave your audience wanting and expecting more

This is crucial to securing a lasting impact. As with many of the examples cited above (the chocolate mousse, the orgasm) you need to leave your audience wanting more of your speech, more of its content, more of your ideas and more of you. This is so that not only will they remember what you said but will also investigate further on the subject, attend future speeches of yours and be more likely to follow up on your call to action. To succeed, you need to know your subject matter very well and know what to leave out of the speech. You also need lots of practice (again!) so that you do it in a subtle, smooth, almost invisible way. The idea is to make your audience aware that the end of your speech is not really the end of your project, idea or passion. To hint that there is much more behind it and that you are willing to share it with them – but not just yet.

As with a good film or book, you treasure those last minutes or seconds (or pages) because you don't want to reach its end. But you also feel a huge sense of excitement and anticipation knowing that this is indeed the end (at least the end for now).

"When you finish your speech, you should always leave an open door. Leave open the possibility of a follow-up speech or conversation with your audience."

While reading this chapter you may have felt that these principles only apply to politicians and professional speakers. But in truth they are applicable to any public speech you give, whether a presentation at work, a meeting you chair for the charity you volunteer with or an appointment with your children's teachers.

To be successful, any public speaking interaction should aim to make an impact through the robustness of its content and its delivery. It must generate further interest in you and what you have to say by creating that sense of craving and further exploration. Ignite their passion and make them want more: more of you and more of your ideas, so that your relationship between your audience and your speech becomes a dynamic process that walks alongside the story of your life – your story.

Plant a Seed

***

Alright, alright, alright…I am getting a bit carried away! And, yes, I can see why this may be difficult to apply to everyday public speaking situations and may seem more relevant for professional public speakers who make a living out of speaking. But just by having this concept in your head and by not revealing all your cards at once, you will create a sense of interest and intrigue that will serve your public speaking and your relationships well.

*'The end of your speech is the beginning of a relationship...
with the audience'*

Brutally Concise Summary of Part 3

And you have done it! You now have read the ten most useful pieces of advice you will ever read. And it has only cost you an hour of your time and a few pounds. What a great deal! Before you read the four ADDITIONAL NOTES (WOW!) that follow, I am going to provide you with a brutal reminder of these last three chapters:

- Keep practising: it's never enough so **Practice** as much as you can.

- Keep **DRESS CODE** in mind: shorts and flip-flops or skirt and high heels, make sure you dress for the moment.

- Keep them hungry and thirsty for more of your speeches, for more of you. **SAVE MATERIAL** for the next speech and conclude with a memorable quote.

The Bonus Material

A Note on Unprepared, Off-the-cuff, Impromptu Speaking

A Note on Speaking Topics

A Note on Special Speeches: The Best Man Speech and Other Potentially Emotional and Embarrassing Occasions

A Note on Humour

A Note on Unprepared, Off-the-cuff, Impromptu Speaking

Most of this book has been written for situations where you have had time to prepare, such as a work meeting, a scheduled speech at a social event or a corporate presentation. I hope that what I am about to say doesn't surprise you or change your opinion about the value of your investment in this book. The book is invaluable and will equip you with the tools to succeed in your public speaking journey. But my experience tells me that a large proportion of the occasions when we will be speaking in public are unexpected, unplanned and even unwanted. But that's the way life happens, and we need to be prepared.

From strangers in the street to friends (and friends of friends) at dinner parties, colleagues at work, your boss in a meeting, your in-laws, your children, your mother, the list is endless. We know, because we've all been there, that life is going to throw us into situations where we are expected to talk, to say something in public and with very little or no time to prepare. These situations can be stressful, uncomfortable and even embarrassing. We often "hate" the person putting us in that position for being outrageously indiscreet and inconsiderate and annoying and stupid (and whatever other adjectives you can think of!).

To be equipped with some basic tips on how to deal with these situations is going to make you feel, look and sound more confident. So here you go:

1. The three-second "say thank you, breathe and think rule". Whenever you find yourself in a situation where you are expected to speak in front of a group and have had no time to think or prepare, the first thing you need to do is to gain some thinking time. A great way to do this is to spend a few seconds thanking the "questioner" for giving you the opportunity to express your view and share your thoughts with the rest of the group on such an interesting and important topic. While a part of your brain does this (I don't know which one!), another part can start plotting and putting together what you want your response to the question

to be. A smile and a two to three second pause is also acceptable and polite and will buy you some extra thinking time, too. Don't panic, just smile, pause, breathe and say "Thank you" to the person for their question.

2. Keep it simple, short and sweet. Hopefully those few initial seconds have given you time to think about one or two things to say. Ideally, you should come up with one positive thing to say about whatever it is you have been asked to talk about. Then try to find another point that gets your audience thinking. Try to share the responsibility of your task by getting them to consider potential negative elements or by posing a rhetorical question for them to ponder.

3. Sum up. If you are able to control your nerves, allow yourself to spend a few seconds to summarise what you have said. Then thank the person who asked the question again and hand it back to him (or to someone else in the group) with a smile or another question for them (!).

'Impromptu speaking happens everywhere: be prepared!'

A Note on Speaking Topics

When faced with the task of speaking in public, one of the key challenges we all face is to know and decide what to say. This is true even when we are told what to talk about. What is my topic, subject, message, content, substance going to be? And the more speaking engagements you do, the tougher finding things to speak about becomes. The primary sources for speaking topics are, in descending order of appeal: yourself, those close to you, and the world around you and its current or future state.

Talk About Yourself

This is always a good idea, whether it is your experience, your career or your family. Because it comes naturally and you have lived it, it makes remembering what you say easier. It also establishes a closer, more personal and deeper connection with the audience. As I've already mentioned in detail in Chapter 3, a story format is always an advantage because it is more engaging and easier for your audience to follow and remember.

As you begin to explore the possibilities of your public speaking profile (and possibly, career) exploit the reserve of personal topics you can draw from, whether a childhood trauma or military service, your first child or your wedding day. The only note of caution on this approach is to link your story to something bigger and more profound than yourself. This allows the audience not only to learn about you but also to take away a lesson that they can apply to their own lives. This can be presented in the form of "a lesson learnt", "the moral of the story" or a thought-provoking reflection on what your story means and how the audience can benefit from it. This link to the listener can either be inserted throughout the speech as you unfold your story or at the end, in the conclusion, for maximum impact. If you choose to do this at the end, allow the conclusion to be a bit longer than the standard conclusion so that the audience has the time to enjoy it, process it and remember it.

Bring In Those Close to You

As seen in Chapter 3, this is also a useful resource when it comes to deciding upon speaking topics. Talking about friends, relatives and colleagues expands your speaking horizons. As long as you ensure there is a meaningful story and message behind the characters it will enrich your speeches and the audience's experience. You could talk about a relative's courage dealing with a terminal illness to either bring awareness about the illness or inspire the audience. Or you could recount a friend's extraordinary achievement in order to try and motivate the audience. It could be just a tale of love and focusing on what matters if you are talking about your children or spouse. As well as making your speech more personal, bringing in people close to you helps you make the point you want to make and achieve your objective more effectively, whether you are aiming to be leading, inspiring or motivating.

Draw From The World Around You

Politics, education, peace and war, poverty, health care, medical research, public speaking itself! Finances, a company, a charity, a president or prime minister (feed your speech with history if you go down this route), public affairs – the list is endless. Just make sure that whatever you choose is relevant and of interest and that you can connect it somehow with the audience's reality and their world for greater attention and impact.

'Your topics, your brand'

A Note on Special Speeches
The Best Man Speech and Other Potentially Emotional and Embarrassing Occasions

A wedding, a funeral, a birthday party, a Christmas party, an office party, an anniversary, a graduation…We are all likely to find ourselves as the speaking centre of attention in one of these scenarios at some point in our lives. If you have been given time to prepare, great! Just follow the advice in the ten preceding chapters. If it is an "off-the-cuff" speech, try and follow the tips in my previous note on impromptu speaking.

Above all, the two key elements to remember are:

*   Keep it short (I would recommend a minimum of three to five minutes and a maximum of 20).

*   Keep it personal (so draw from your own feelings as much as possible).

Pauses will be needed more than ever in these speeches to compose yourself and recover and also to allow your audience to taste the emotions and process them as your speech progresses. Ideally, these speeches should be humorous too, so more on that now.

'Short and sweet.'

A Note on Humour

Not everyone is created equal. Some people are funny, some aren't. But here's the good news – there is a difference between being funny and being humorous. Whilst not everybody is funny (I am not) everybody can use humour in a speech, or any other situation, by offering a human, self-deprecating, alternative, unexpected, different, unique perspective on an event, character or story. And that is what is required when it comes to humorous public speaking.

If you are a funny person and can make people laugh, then do. The audience will engage with you more and will feel more relaxed.

If you are not naturally funny, trying to be so may backfire, so don't. You don't have to. Instead try and dilute the tone and the seriousness of your speech by narrating something unusual that happened to you. Or even add an embarrassing anecdote that you are prepared to share with the audience. It will make you look and sound more human, more approachable, more accessible, more personal – and more interesting. Doing this at the beginning of a speech is particularly useful as a way to catch the audience's attention, get everybody to relax (including yourself) and set the tone for the rest of the speech.

Don't overdo it, as your message may lose impact or credibility. Unless, of course, the only objective of the speech is to make people laugh!

'Not all men/women are born funny: be humorous instead'

AFTERWORD

And that's it, the end.

I hope you feel inspired and energised to continue learning and to apply what you have learnt to your everyday verbal interactions. I do genuinely hope that you have found it useful.

If the contents of the book aren't what you were hoping for, I would love to hear your recommendations for improvement. If you like what you have read and learnt and want more, the good news is that I will continue to write more titles on the subject of public speaking because it is…everywhere!

Until then, for now, thank you!

AFTERTHOUGHT

It may have occurred to you, the reader, that in this book I haven't covered (at least not directly) the management of public speaking nerves and the use of written notes, although I have alluded to both briefly throughout the text.

Nerves

In relation to nerves, I refer you to the LinkedIn article I wrote on that subject which you will find on my LinkedIn profile www.linkedin.com/in/carlosgimenopsf. The article is an initial reflection on a big subject – and I am very happy to have a direct conversation with any readers who may wish to talk about it.

Written Notes

As for written notes, the goal is to reach a level of comfort and proficiency that allows you to go solo and speak without notes. But that's the destination. The journey will see you, with help from this book, progress through various stages. You will go from using a full transcript of your words, which you will have in front of you when you speak, to an abridged version that you use as a reference, then to just a few cards or bullet points that will be there in case your mind goes blank, something our brains sometimes like doing. My advice is to practice in advance as much as you can, so that you don't need to rely on notes, and even if you have notes with you, avoid reading from them. They're just there as a tool to rescue you in case of a crisis.

The more you have prepared, the more you use storytelling (or *storyology*) and the more you believe in what you say the less you will need to have notes with you.

If you would like to discuss with me any of these topics in more detail, please reach out to me on social media or on carlos@publicspeakingfor.com.

AFTERLIFE

No, this is not an esoteric or metaphysical note. This is just a note to say that the life of this book starts now, when you have finished it. The book and its lessons will travel with you to those occasions when you need them, and I recommend that you re-read them, re-interpret them and continue to practice them for months and years to come. There is therefore an afterlife to this book which starts with you and the learning journey you begin/continue now.